ZEN COLOURING

THE ULTIMATE COLLECTION

THE GUILD OF MASTER CRAFTSMAN PUBLICATIONS

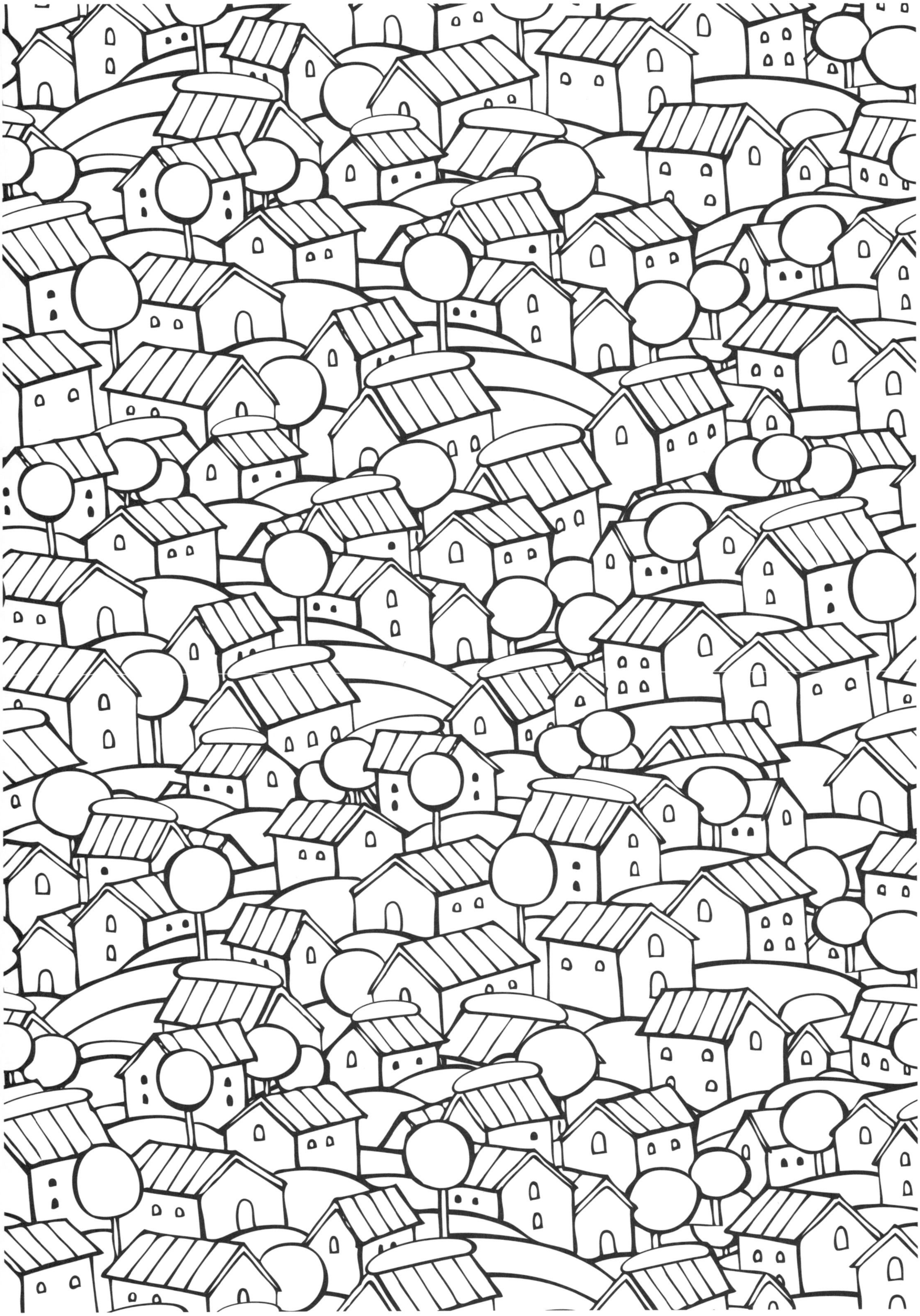

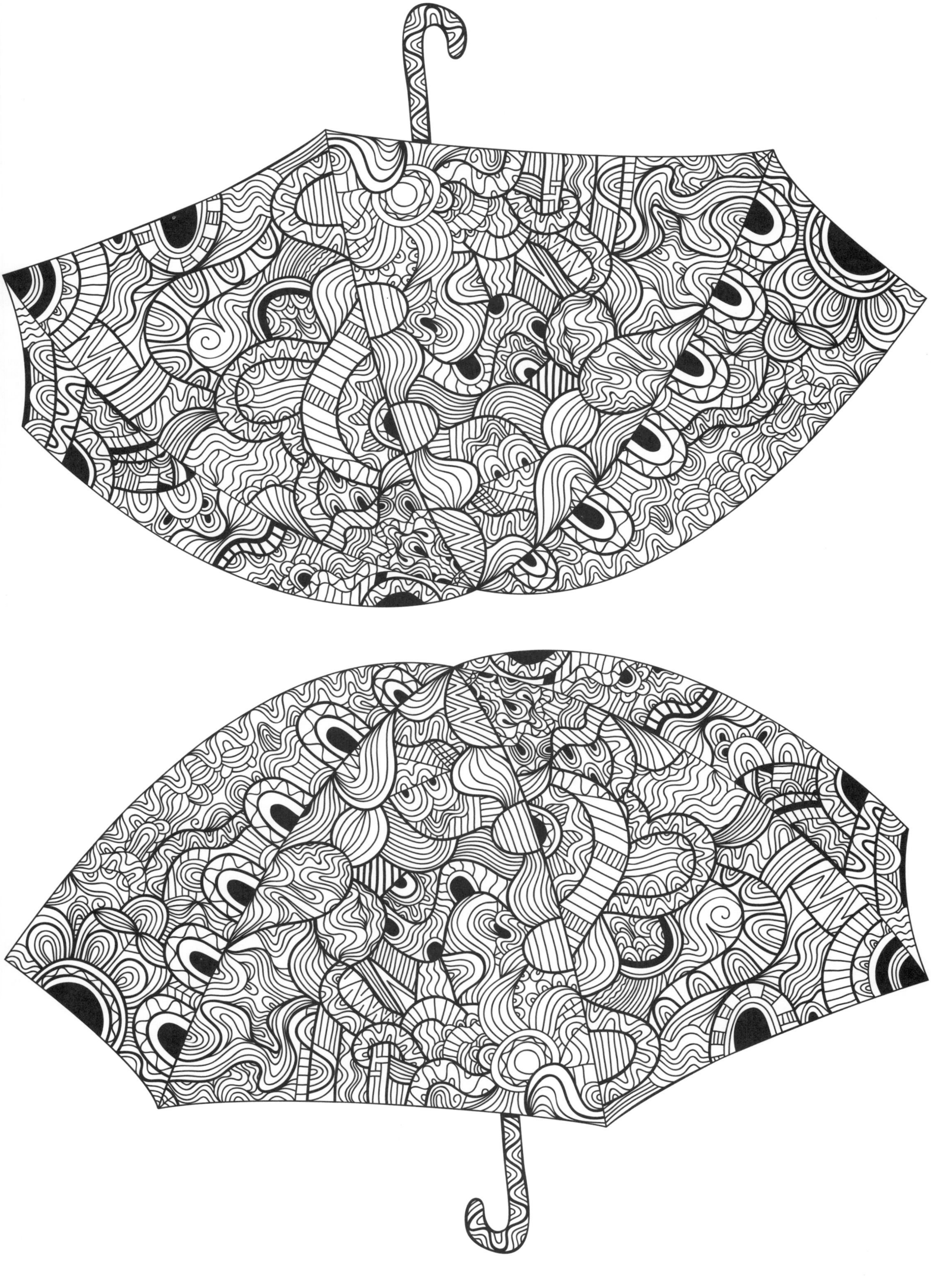

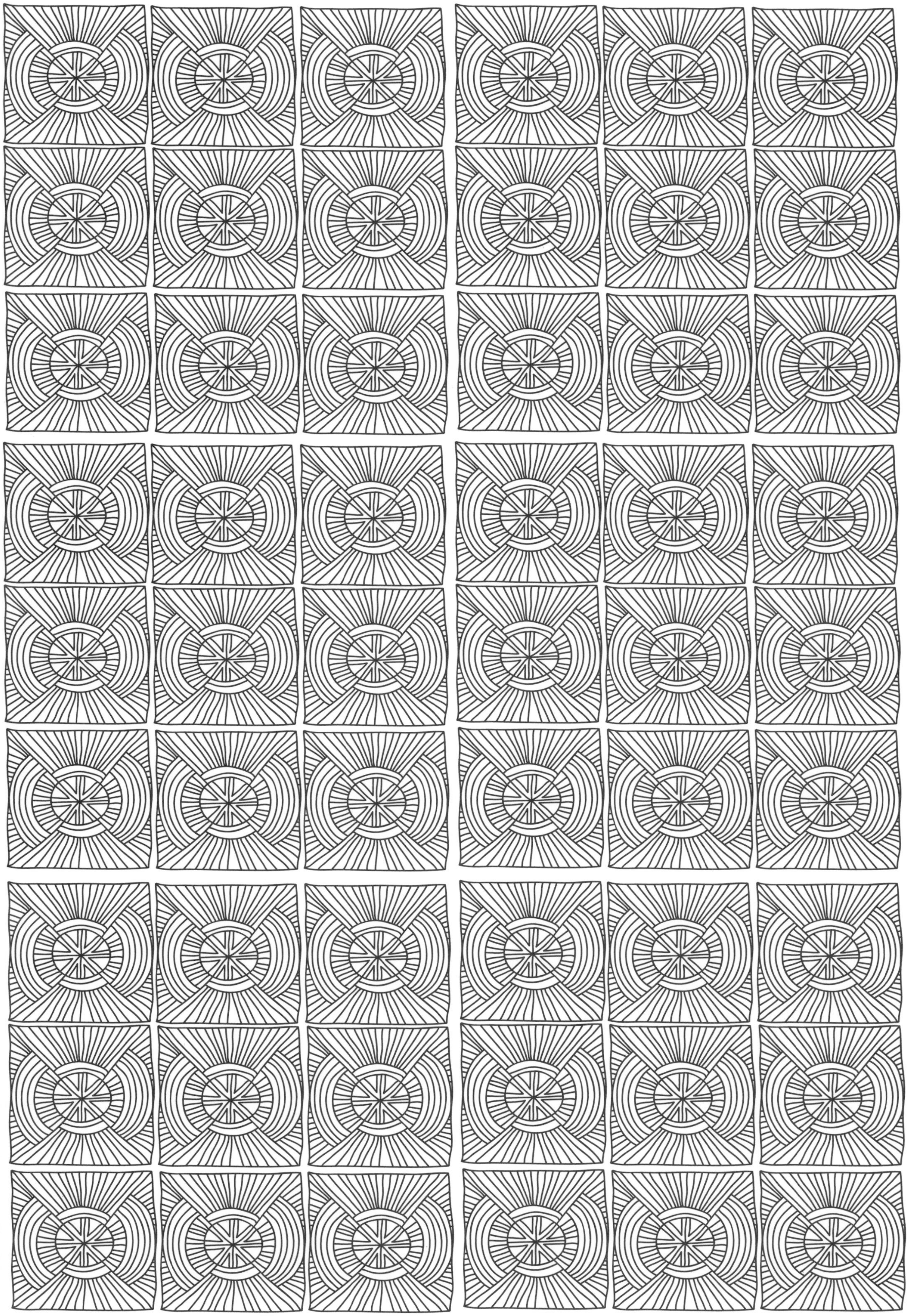

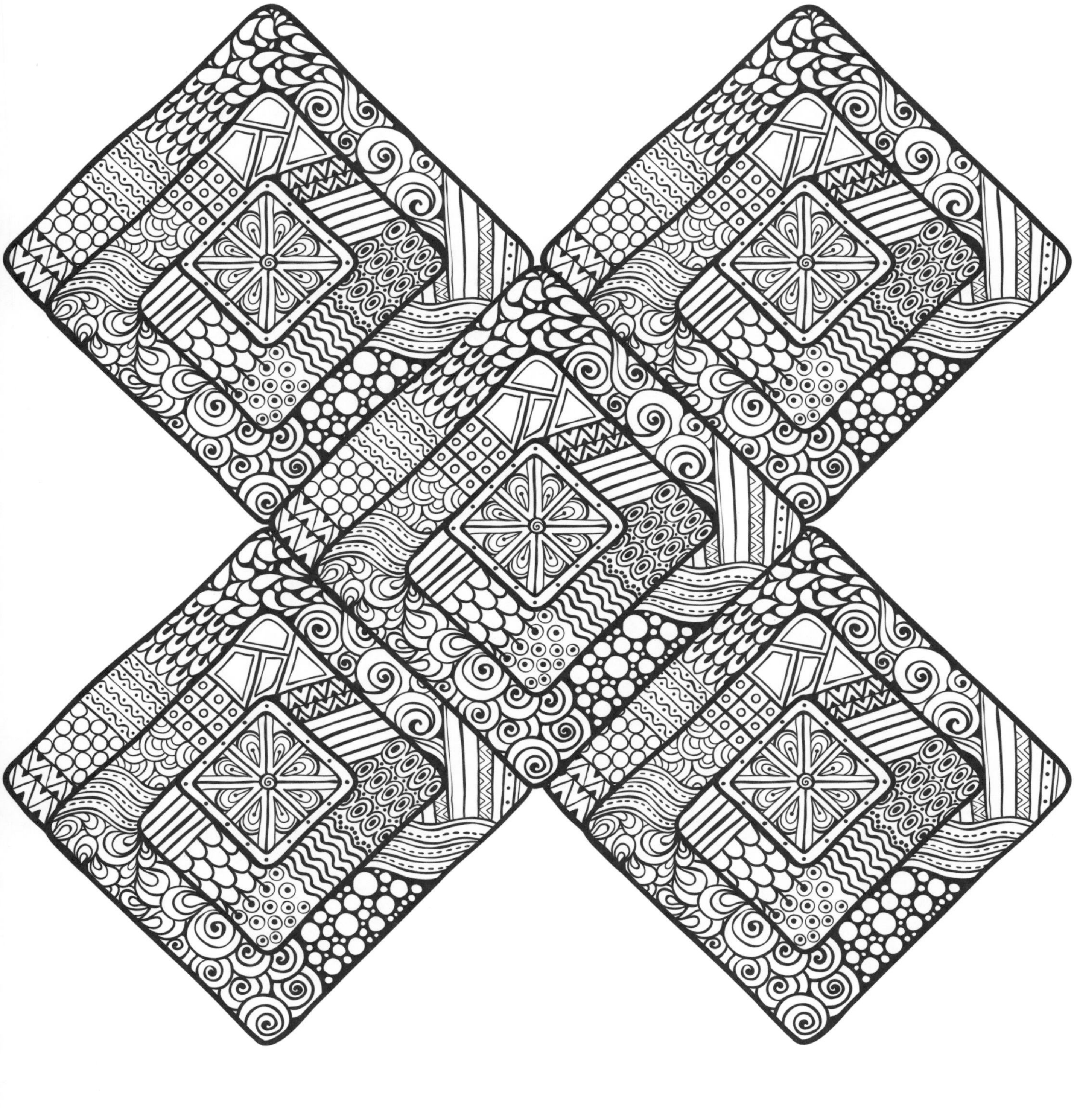

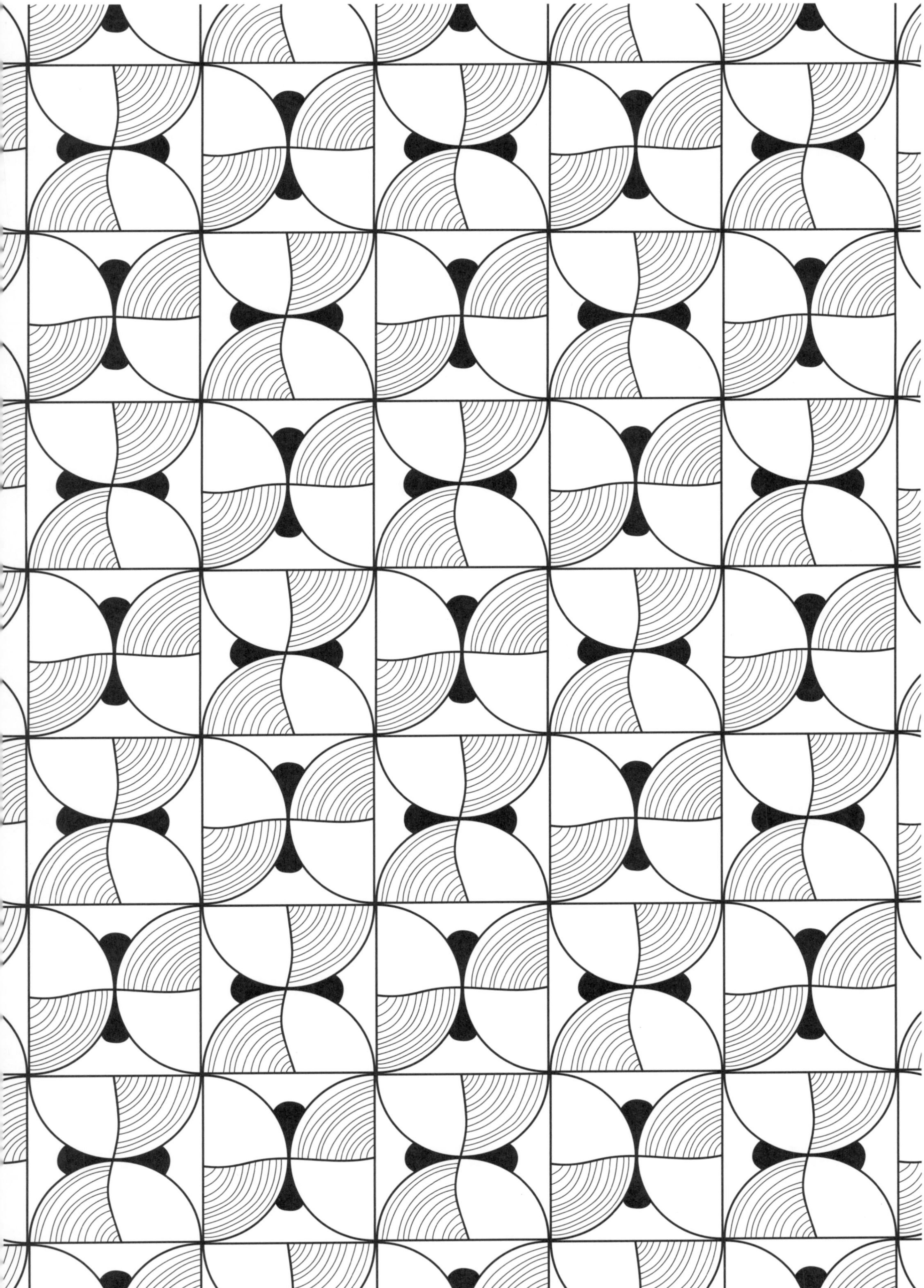

To place an order, or to request a catalogue, contact:

GMC Publications Ltd,
Castle Place, 166 High Street,
Lewes, East Sussex, BN7 1XU,
United Kingdom

Tel: +44 (0)1273 488005

www.gmcbooks.com